BARTHOLOMEW ROBERTS' JUSTICE

JEREMY MCLEAN

No part of this book may be reproduced, scanned, or distributed in any printed or electronic form without written permission from the author of this novel.

POINTS OF SAIL
PUBLISHING

Points of Sail Publishing
P.O. Box 30083 Prospect Plaza
FREDERICTON, New Brunswick
E3B 0H8, Canada

Edited by Ethan James Clarke
http://silverjay-editing.com/

Cover Design by Kit Foster

This is a work of fiction. Any similarity to persons, living or dead, is purely coincidental… Or is it?

Copyright © 2015 Jeremy McLean
All rights reserved.
ISBN: 0-9878095-8-X
ISBN-13: 978-0-9878095-8-2

ACKNOWLEDGEMENTS

Big thanks go to my friends and family as usual. I can't keep writing without my support team behind me.

Ethan James Clarke is a great editor and a far better writer than I. He's a great help in taking my novel to the next level. If you're in need of editing, check out http://silverjay-editing.com

TABLE OF CONTENTS

1: Bartholomew the Bear 1
2: A Short and Merry Life.. 19
3: Eye of the Beholder... 30
4: God Provides.. 43
5: The Pirate Priest.. 55

1. BARTHOLOMEW THE BEAR

Bartholomew Roberts, the pirate, sat at a table in a bar with some sailors. He was spinning a tale about a recent expedition which saw him and his crew hitting a storm. The tale was as tall as him, given that the goal was to gain their trust.

"I tell you, men, the storm was like none I had seen before. It came and left like a spectre before anyone noticed what was happening. We have two ships and we're lucky they're still with us," Roberts stated before taking a swig of his drink.

The hovel he found himself in was a lively tavern with all manner of immoral men and women finding solace under its roof. The smell of unkempt bodies, spilled ale and wine permeated the surroundings, as did the laughter and talk of general festivity.

"Lucky is not runnin' into no pirates after yer run-in. That's lucky," one of the men commented.

Roberts smiled. "Yea, I'm thankful for that as well." His smile faded. "You've been attacked recently, I take it?" he asked, his melodic Welsh accent undercutting his seriousness.

"Ay, last week on the way here. Took my whole shipment of silks and my savings. Thanks to that I can't even afford another shipment. I need to take on a loan just to keep sailing."

He shook his head. "Tch, tch. Isn't that just the way?

Bartholomew Roberts' Justice

What about you gents? Business going smoothly, or are you meeting storms like this gentleman…?" He gestured to the first man with his mug.

"Gerald."

"This man, Gerald, and I?"

"I was shipping ten tonnes of rum," another man at the table explained, "and one tonne of spices. Spices got waterlogged because of some fault in the barrels and the rum burned after one of my men got into it and had an accident. I made sure he had another 'accident' later on." He took a long drink, and he had had one too many already. His nose and cheeks were peach red. "An' now, word spread that my luck is bad and my crew worse, so I got nowhere prospecting."

"Such a shame," Roberts said. *Nothing to steal from you, that is the shame…* He then turned to the third man in the group he'd pulled together from the patrons in the tavern. "What of you, sir? You seem awfully quiet. How are the seas treating you?"

The third man was young, had his hair tied back, and wore a new-looking sailor uniform. He was dressed down, as this wasn't the sort of place one would wear a uniform, but it was clear he was part of some company.

"Things are going well, sorry to say for you gents," he answered in a proper British accent.

Roberts noticed a slight twinge on the corner of the man's lips. He pointed at the man. "Oh! I see that smile. Come now, you old dog, you're holding back on us. You're about to have a payday soon, aren't you?" he speculated with a big grin on his face.

The gentleman couldn't hold back a grin of his own, Roberts' being as contagious as it was. "I shouldn't say."

The charismatic Welshman mocked a frown and then

smiled again. "Now you've teased us again. You can't tell half the story and then forgo the rest. The curiosity is liable to eat us alive. Isn't that right, gents?"

The others at the table joined in with Roberts' boisterousness. Together they chided the sailor into telling the whole story, even though he hadn't really said anything to begin with.

"Alright," the man finally conceded. "I do not wish to boast, so I will only say I recently acquired quite a lucrative contract with the East India Company to ship stock west."

With the mention of that name, the other sailors' eyes and ears perked. Roberts whistled. "Sounds profitable indeed. When are you due to ship out?"

"After our ship is cleaned, in near abouts two days."

"And you're sailing the *Decadence*? Three sails, thirty guns?" he asked.

The man nodded. "That would be the one."

"Bartholomew?" someone called.

Roberts turned around to see one of his crewmates timidly approaching, but nonetheless with urgency in his eyes. He waved for his crewmate to join him, but the man shook his head and beckoned his captain over.

"Excuse me for a moment, gentlemen," he said before rising from the table and walking over to his crewman. "What is it? I'm in the middle of finding our next plunder."

The man was wringing his hat in his hands, nervousness creeping through. "It's bad, Captain. None of the men know what to do."

Roberts held his hands up. "Calm. Breathe. From the beginning now."

The crewmate glanced about to make sure no one was

listening. "Hank, a few of the commanders, and seven of the crew were taken from a tavern."

"Taken? By whom?"

"The local militia. They're being held in the prison on the other side of town."

Roberts rubbed his chin and muttered a curse under his breath. "Head back to the ship. I'll handle it."

"Sir?" the crewmate questioned, brow cocked.

"I've seen the prison. It's small and only manned by a few people. With the daylight waning, I shouldn't have a problem rescuing the boys. Any more people and we would draw suspicion. Tell the crew I will be back by midnight."

"Yes, Captain," the man stammered before heading out the tavern's swinging door.

Roberts returned to the table, took the last drink of his ale, and placed a note on the table. "Unfortunately, I must be leaving now. Gentlemen, it has been a pleasure."

The captains lifted their glasses to him and said goodbye as he left.

Roberts checked his person quickly to ensure he was prepared for what he was about to do. *Pistol, sword, everything in order. Wait, where is my…* He touched his back pocket, the same pocket that once held a Bible he'd owned for quite a time. That familiar leather book used to be a staple in his back pocket, but was no longer there. *Half a year and still I reach for that book. Davey Jones must be finished reading it by now.*

He put his thoughts back on his crew and moved on towards the prison. Day was starting to leave the port town, and the sun on the horizon shone light on the harbour and at Roberts' back. The golden glow reflected in the wood and stone of the houses as he passed by, and cast his shadow larger than life on the walls and alleys. Seven feet tall as he was, the shadow he cast was great indeed.

He reached the prison at one side of town, and assessed its fortifications. It was a stone building, not really much of a prison, but slightly bigger than all the other buildings in the town. He had heard the prison held close to one hundred prisoners, but at most only twenty guards of the militia were present at a time, and that was during the day.

Directly in front of the prison stood a five-foot raised platform with a wooden hanging beam in the middle. A man already long dead was suspended in the air by a noose. The smell emanating from the body was sickly, not quite at the point of decay, but fouled by excrement. His body was limp and his arms were tied behind his back. Below his neck, his skin was pale; red marks could be seen surrounding the rope tight around his neck, and his tongue involuntarily stuck out of his mouth and had turned purplish. His eyes were still open, bloodshot and staring at Roberts in the eerie way the dead peer at everyone. A placard hung around his shoulders, resting on his stomach, which read "Pirate."

Roberts couldn't help but stare back at the man, wondering what his true crime was, and how he'd ended up being executed. *I will not let my men suffer the same fate.* He had a brief inclination to pray for the dead man, but shook his head and kept walking.

He sauntered around the buildings surrounding the prison. No other buildings were very close to the prison, which allowed him a good line of sight to view it from all angles. Other men and women were still walking about the village, so he was able to blend in while examining his target.

There were two entrances, one at the front with the hanging podium, and another at the back. Each was guarded by two armed men in blue uniforms similar to those worn by the British Royal Navy, but cut off at the elbow.

Though no houses were close by, the prison was in plain view. *I won't be able to enter without drawing unwanted attention. I must find another way.*

When Roberts took another walk round the prison, he noticed a few guards leaving. He observed the men talking and laughing with each other while walking.

They must be finishing their shift. If I can take one of their uniforms I could walk through the front door of the prison…

He tailed the three guards. The people of the town were beginning to disperse as night drew in, and he was able to easily follow them. After a moment, one of the men separated from the group and entered a side street. Roberts followed the lone man.

The guard walked through the side street until he reached a house and turned to enter. He turned his gaze in Roberts' direction. Roberts missed a step. The guard tensed.

There are still people in the streets. I cannot make a move yet. He regained his composure and resumed his stride.

"Keep up the good work, mate," he said as he passed the guard.

The other man nodded as Roberts passed by. He could still feel the guard's gaze on his back. He turned the corner at the end of the street and continued walking to the next side street.

Roberts laid his back against the wall and took a deep breath, wiping sweat off his brow. He pushed himself off the wall and approached the house the guard had entered. At the back of the house there was an exit and an alley to access the side, which he entered.

The side of the house had a few low double-hung louvre windows and the shutters were open. He went up close to one of them, keeping his body close to the wall of the house. Voices travelled out of the open shutters.

"… prisoners give you any trouble today?" s female voice asked.

"Nah, the new ones ain't any trouble," a male voice responded. "The new 'uns are positively jovial."

He must be talking about Hank and the others.

"They're scheduled for execution on the morrow, yet behave better than the local drunks. It's like they're not afraid of the noose. It's unsettling."

"Aww, well I know something to help settle ye," the woman replied.

Sounds of kissing filtered from behind the screen, then the sound of footsteps moving further to the back of the house, and then a door closing. *Here's my chance.*

He moved closer to the front of the house and peered in through one of the shutters. He was looking into the living room of the guard's house, and could see the blue coat resting on a chair next to a table. The chair was too far from the window, so he somehow had to enter the house to get the uniform.

He glanced to the ends of the alley. It was dark, and most everyone was indoors at this hour. The house next to the guard's home was dark, presumably because no one was home, which made things easier for him.

Roberts lifted the window shutter as far as it could go, then climbed up into the opening. He took a moment to check the inside again, and, not seeing any residents in the living room, he continued his entrance. He was not a small man, and so the window was a tight squeeze. He could feel the grating of the shutters digging into his back. The giant took a deep breath and sucked in his gut. He moved his arms up and into the living room, and pushed against the siding of the window as he shimmied his torso through. After a moment of struggle, he was halfway through, and only his legs were dangling outside.

The chair was almost within reach now. *If I can just catch the uniform I won't have to enter all the way.* He extended his arms in front of him. His upper body started to fall forward and his legs flew up in the air. He planted his hand on the floor and then spread his legs out to keep his balance on the window sill.

Roberts reached for the chair, but it was still an inch away. He swatted at it in an attempt to get closer, but it wasn't helping. He kept shuffling forward precariously on the windowsill. The Welshman managed to get one finger on the edge of the chair and clenched his teeth as he pushed down with all his might. The chair moved forward ever so slowly, and with his other hand he was able to grab the coat.

After removing the coat, the chair became a lot lighter, and he didn't have a proper grip on it. It fell through his fingers and made a loud snap as it hit the floor. He cringed and then rushed to pull himself out of the window.

He drew himself up against the wall of the house and flattened against it. He listened intently as he held his breath with the uniform clenched in his hand. After a moment of no door opening, he let out his breath. No one seemed to hear him.

He pulled off his top and attempted to put on the

guard's uniform. The uniform was tight across his broad chest, and he was forced to tug on the arm to finally get it to fit. As he tugged, the fabric frayed with a loud rip.

He tensed and stood up straight. He turned as best as he could to inspect himself, and was disheartened. It had ripped on the arms and the bottom of the sides. The uniform normally went halfway down the forearm if it fit, but in Roberts' case it only reached a little over his elbow. His hairy arms were showing, as were the hairs on his chest through the obviously stressed buttons. It was constricting on the arms and chest, and he had a hard time even breathing in the outfit.

It will have to do. Just act the part, and the rest will come together.

He looked up to see a young boy staring at him in the street at the end of the alley. By his snickering the child had been there for some time.

"Run along now, young one, before I teach you some manners," Roberts warned with the back of his palm raised.

The boy laughed and ran off.

Roberts moved deliberately towards the street and back to the prison. He kept his back straight and his gut sucked in as he walked. Along the way, the few people who were still wandering the streets gave him odd looks when he passed. By the time he reached the prison, he was sweating and his arms were beginning to tingle from poor circulation.

He marched up to the doors of the prison, going over what he could say to the men guarding to allow him entrance. *I will tell them I am late for my shift, apologize, and walk through. That will be the simplest.*

When he approached the doors, he half opened his

mouth, ready to give his story, but the guards simply moved aside to allow him entrance. Roberts missed a step, peered warily at the men in front of him, and then entered the prison. They seemed to pay him no heed as he passed.

Perhaps this costume doesn't look as tight as I thought.

He found himself in a not-so-great hall. Empty tables and chairs sat in the middle of the room, and racks next to doors on either side of the room held spare weapons. Straight in front of him was another door as well.

He decided to head straight, and went through the door. In the next room was a long hallway with prison cells lining either side. A pair of armed guards were talking with each other in the middle of the hallway.

He glanced back and forth, examining those in the cells as he roamed. The quality of the cells left a lot to be desired. They were small and cramped, with too many people stuffed inside. The smell of faeces and other bodily odours filled the area. The prisoners were loud and some tried to grasp Roberts as he passed by, but he was out of reach.

Each cell was secured with iron bars and thick stone separated the small quarters from each other. There were no windows or openings to allow air to enter, thus the smell lingered with no way of escaping, just as the prisoners did.

As he passed the guards, they nodded to him, once again giving him only a cursory glance and nothing more.

Any in their right mind would think there's something strange; my arms are turning white, I'm sweating seawater and this uniform is splitting at the seams. I suppose I shouldn't look this gift horse in the mouth.

At the end of the hallway a staircase led to the second

floor of the prison. He checked the cells at the back before moving on up the stairs.

From his examination, the prison had only two floors, but it felt smaller on the inside. He was sure there were more rooms with prisoners, as he could see doors on either end of the hall. He first entered the room nearest the front of the prison.

Inside the room was a single prison cell, larger than the rest by far, with a small window at the top covered with iron bars and doors on either side like the entrance of the prison. Roberts was taken aback when he saw his crew right in front of him. Some were playing a game of cards on the cell floor while Hank was being questioned by one of the guards.

"I'll ask you again, what ship are you with and what is the name of your captain?"

Hank sighed, and then glanced briefly at the door where he saw his captain. His eyes shot open for a split second before he regained his composure. Hank returned his attention to the guard questioning him.

"I'll tell you again: we belong to no ship and answer to no captain."

"Three times you've denied having a captain, but I know this is not the truth."

A crow perched in the window near the cell and called out, drawing the attention of the crew and the guard. The crew then glanced to the door and noticed their captain.

Roberts put his finger to his mouth to silence the crew before they cried out. They returned to their game of cards, and acted as if nothing was different. The guard resumed questioning Hank, none the wiser.

Roberts closed the door and silently moved behind the guard. The Welsh giant wrapped his massive arm around the man's neck, and covered his mouth with his palm. The guard struggled and pulled against him, but it was no use. Roberts was far stronger than the smaller man. The pressure against the guard's neck cut off his air; his thrashing slowed as the seconds passed until his arms and legs went limp. Roberts slowly set the man on the floor, then grabbed the keys off his belt.

He took the keys to the cage his crew was set in, and began trying each key on the iron lock.

"Captain, you are a sight for sore eyes," Hank said. "I thought we were gonna be left behind."

Roberts gestured at the card game. "You didn't seem too concerned."

Hank glanced back to the cards, then to his captain again. "Can't let 'em see us sweat, now can we? We have reputations to uphold."

"True enough." With the next key, the iron bars were opened.

The crew exited the cage and thanked their captain profusely. Smiles abounded on all the men's faces, and there was much rejoicing.

"Now, how about we leave this place?" Roberts suggested.

"There's a storage area in that room with spare uniforms we can don." Hank pointed to a door on the side of the room.

"The guards here seem rather inept, so I don't believe we would have issues regardless, but it's better to be safe."

Roberts used the keys once again to open the storage room, and the crew entered.

Inside the room were weapons, piles of clothes, and supplies for repairs. The clothes were not simply uniforms, but also what appeared to be clothes from former and possibly current prisoners.

The crew rummaged through the clothes to find uniforms they could wear. Roberts kept watch at the door. Hank took the clothes from the guard, and then locked the man in the cage before changing into the uniform.

"Sure am glad you came by, Captain."

"Of course I would. I couldn't leave you all here to be hung. What kind of a captain leaves his men behind?"

"You'd be surprised."

"I suppose it has happened to you before?" Roberts asked as he glanced to see his crew still changing.

"Too many times to count, I reckon. The types of men attracted to this life aren't always the most loyal. You're different, though, just like Davis. That's why most of us wanted you as captain: you inspire loyalty in others."

Roberts' face was melancholic for a moment as his thoughts turned to his former captain who'd introduced him to piracy. After a moment he raised his brow with a sly smile. "Most?"

"Aye, most. You can't please everyone. I say don't try, it's the majority that counts anyway."

Roberts smiled. "True enough."

Hank finished changing, and the clothes he had been able to procure were a much better fit than Roberts'. The crew finished around the same time, and returned to the first room.

"So, where to now, Captain?"

"We can escape through the back. Two guards are covering the exit, but it shouldn't be hard to knock them out." The crew nodded. "Follow me."

Roberts opened the door to the prison's second-floor hallway, and after a cursory glance to check for guards, he stepped inside. He guided his crew past the other cells with prisoners still locked in cages.

The prisoners seemed to know something was wrong and became more agitated. They yelled and reached out to the pirates as they passed.

When they reached the stairs, Roberts looked down to the lower level to see the guards trying to silence the prisoners. The commotion on the second floor transitioned below, affording him and his crew an opportunity.

He rushed down the steps and opened the door to the back room of the prison while he watched the two guards. He motioned for his crew to go through the door while the guards were distracted. One by one, the group of fifteen casually went through the door without the prison guards taking notice.

Inside, the back room of the prison was a mirror to the front entrance, complete with weapons on racks off to the sides. Some of the crew grabbed weapons.

Roberts closed the door behind him. "Don't take the weapons," he whispered. "When I was watching the guards, none left the prison with weapons. If we are carrying any when we leave it will arouse suspicion if any locals see us."

The crew followed their captain's advice and returned the weapons. Roberts motioned for Hank to join him at the back exit.

He placed his hand on the door and glanced at Hank. His crewmate nodded. He opened the door, and in front of them were the two guards Roberts had seen when he circled the prison.

Roberts and Hank both grabbed one of the guards, and pulled them inside. Roberts closed the door with his foot while slamming the man he grabbed against the wall.

Jeremy McLean

He held his hand against the man's mouth so he couldn't scream. The man muffled something as his eyes shifted back and forth trying to make sense of what was happening. Before he could act, Roberts punched him hard in the stomach and released his grip on the guard. The guard doubled over in pain, and he struggled to breathe. He gripped Roberts' leg, his mouth wide open in a struggle to shout, but instead only saliva escaped and hit the floor of the prison. The man's eyes soon shut as he fell unconscious.

Roberts turned his attention to Hank, who also took care of the guard he grabbed. The two were both breathing hard, moreso from the rush of the fight than the physical exertion.

Hank looked at his captain, and after a few breaths he started laughing. Roberts cocked his brow. "Captain, your uniform has seen better days."

He examined himself, extending his arms and seeing what Hank noticed. The uniform was truly gone now. The seams across the arm all the way up the biceps and underarms were torn, as were the sides of the stomach.

"On the positive side, at least now I can breathe properly," Roberts said with a laugh, which the crew joined in. "Alright everyone, let's walk out of here in groups of two or three and split up. We'll meet back at the ship." The crew nodded and they all left the prison.

Roberts joined Hank and they made their way back to the harbour. It was well into the night so the streets were mostly empty. Any people they did meet did not seem to think them out of the ordinary and paid them no heed. The two made it back to the *Royal Rover* and *Fortune* unscathed and undetected.

After a half hour, all the remaining crewmates who

had been imprisoned returned to the ships.

"We've escaped prison for one more day, thanks to you, Roberts." Hank let out a sigh and wiped sweat off his brow.

"We should keep it that way. It would be best to stay on the ship and not venture into town for the time being." Hank nodded. "I suppose I should have asked why you all were arrested in the first place. Do the authorities know we're pirates?"

Hank shook his head. "No, no. It's rather funny, actually. One of the crewmates got into a brawl with someone they shouldn't have, an official of some sort. Before long the whole saloon was in a tussle and the official had us arrested. He kept yelling that we'll be hung for what we did, but I imagine he wasn't very serious. One of the crewmates not captured must have taken it seriously for you to be here." He chuckled.

Roberts didn't laugh. "I believe the official was very serious. The guard I followed to steal this uniform from mentioned that you were to be hung on the morrow."

Hank stopped laughing and gave Roberts a grim, questioning look. He simply nodded to his friend's silent question. "Oh my."

This time Roberts had a hearty laugh. "You almost died, and all you say is 'oh my.' My friend you are either very brave or very much in shock."

"Perhaps a little of both," Hank suggested. After a moment to catch his breath, he found the humour in the situation.

The two joined the rest of the crew below deck, and they celebrated their newly recovered freedom. Stories of Roberts' bravery circulated as quickly as the booze and laughter that night.

Jeremy McLean

The next day, news was surprisingly quiet about the previous night's escape. The pirates heard no whispers about fifteen missing prisoners who escaped the noose, and no officials seemed to be on the lookout for tavern brawlers on the run from justice. However, there was one rumour circulating involving the prison, but not one Roberts, or any really, could have expected.

Roberts and Hank were on the top deck of the *Royal Rover* when they heard the news. A crewman ran up the gangplank, but was out of breath.

"Is something the matter, man? You look as if you've seen an apparition."

"It's about the prison, Captain," the crewmate said between breaths. "I've heard word on something happening there, though I tell you truthfully I'm not quite understanding it."

Roberts and Hank glanced at each other. "Well, let's hear it then."

The crewmate nodded as he took the last few breaths he needed to get back to normal. "No word on escapees, but they say some of the guards were attacked by a bear in a blue suit in the night. The same night we escaped."

Roberts was taken aback. "A bear?"

He nodded. "Yes, Captain. A bear. What do ye figure it means?"

Hank let out a laugh. Roberts and the crewmate looked at him as if he were mad. "It means our captain here is a bit too hairy around the arms, that's what it means."

Roberts shook his head. "You can't possibly…" He raised a brow.

Hank was acting giddy, snickering at his own thoughts. "Bartholomew the Bear has quite the nice ring to it." He

Bartholomew Roberts' Justice

gripped Roberts' shoulder for support as he burst into fits of laughter.

Roberts' face was stone. "You must swear to me the crew will not hear a word of this." He turned to the crewmate who'd brought them the news, and pointed at him menacingly. "Swear to me."

"I'm quite sorry, Captain," Hank said, regaining his composure, but with the hint of his mood dripping from his tone of voice. "This simply cannot be something the crew misses out on."

Hank went below deck to share the story of Bartholomew the Bear with the crew. Roberts shook his head, but couldn't resist smiling himself at the foolishness of the story.

From that day forward, whenever the story was retold, it was with much more laughter, and greater emphasis placed on Roberts' appearance rather than his courage. The name Bartholomew the Bear stuck with the crew not simply as a jest, but also as a source of encouragement. No matter what happened to his crew, the Bear would be there for them.

2. A SHORT AND MERRY LIFE

Walter Kennedy sat slumped on a stool in a tavern, a nearly empty glass loosely in his hands. "More whiskey," he demanded.

The taverner apologized to another customer he was talking with, then looked over at Walter, but did not move an inch. "Your money ran out. Unless ye got more, ye don' get more."

"Tch."

The taverner waved at Walter and shook his head, then returned to talking with his paying customers.

Walter tipped the glass back until it and his face were nearly vertical. The last few drops of his drink snaked their way across the inside of the glass to his tongue. His nose was engulfed in the mouth of the glass, and the smell of the whiskey filled his nostrils. For a brief moment, through watching of the beads of alcohol and the smell, it was just Walter and the drink, and all other thoughts were drowned away. When the beads were gone, and he put the glass back on the table, the thoughts flooded back.

His fault I have no money. If I was captain, we'd have more money than we'd know how to spend.

The sounds of laughter, talking, music, and clinking glasses pounded in his ears. He'd drunk enough to make himself tired, but not enough to suppress the noise. He heard the door open, letting in fresh air and more noise from outside, but he didn't care to see who wandered in.

Someday he'll get what's comin' to him.

The person who entered walked over to where Walter was sitting and placed a hand on his shoulder. He turned his head around and noticed Bartholomew Roberts in front of him.

Speak of the Devil. He chuckled.

"We must leave, Walter. We're setting sail tomorrow and we need you and the crew sobered up by then."

He shook Roberts' hand off his shoulder and turned back around. "I'll be there."

There was a brief pause before Roberts turned him around again. "I want you back on the ship now, Walter. You've finished your drink. You're a commander now and you must set an example for your Commons."

Walter clenched his jaw and gritted his teeth. "I said I'll be there."

Roberts sighed and grabbed him by the arm, pulling him up off the stool. He wasn't strong enough to resist the seven-foot beast in front of him. He saw the patrons staring at the spectacle, sneering at a grown man being treated as a child.

"Get offa' me, ye bastard," he seethed.

Walter planted his feet on the ground and twisted away, causing Roberts' fingers to slip. He lost his footing and fell into one of the patrons, then to the ground.

He climbed back to his feet quickly, seeing that the man he fell on top of spilled his drink all over himself, and was giving him the evil eye. He backed away towards the door of the tavern. The man rose to his feet; his teeth were clenched and his fist was in a ball.

"Get back to the ships, Walter," Roberts commanded. "I'll handle this."

Walter turned and left. *Have fun, Roberts.*

He sauntered back to the ships. By the time he arrived back to the *Fortune* the drink was no longer affecting him, and he felt sober. He boarded the *Fortune* and entered the crew cabin below deck. Along the way he motioned for certain crewmates to join him. He and three others advanced to the back of the crew cabin where two crewmates were lounging and talking.

One of the crewmates' head and face were fully shaved, and he had a tattoo covering half his face. He was cleaning his nails with a large knife when Walter and the men approached.

"Ethan," Walter said to the tattooed man.

Ethan nodded to him. "Welcome back. Have yer fill, did ye?"

"Not hardly. Sit, gents. We 'ave much to discuss." Walter and the three crewmates sat down with the other two on barrels, boxes, and chairs. The Irishman glanced around to make sure there were no prying eyes or perked ears. "Roberts is becoming a problem. Where are we on votes?"

Ethan laughed. "No change since weeks a'fore. Long as Roberts keeps bringing in the money he'll always 'ave people on his side."

"How do we change that then?" Walter asked.

"Not by drinkin' till ye piss yer pants every day, that's fer sure," Ethan jabbed.

"Yer one ta talk, ye bastard."

Ethan shrugged and smiled. "Why don't ye just kill 'im?"

Walter quickly shook his head. "No, no. We can't kill him. I don't want him dead. I simply don't want him to be captain."

Bartholomew Roberts' Justice

"Why ye want him out so bad, then?"

"I thought it was obvious." He looked at his companions, who all gave him looks of confusion. "*I* want to be captain."

Ethan laughed all the harder this time. The other men nervously joined in the laughter. "Wait, yer serious?"

Walter folded his arms. "Yea, of course. I would make a great captain. Better'n Roberts."

"Then tell me, Captain, what makes ye so great? What do ye bring ta tha table that Roberts don't?"

Walter leaned back against the many eyes staring at him, waiting for a response. He could feel sweat beginning to fall across the side of his face. "Well, I can navigate," he lied.

"So can Roberts," Ethan replied, leaning over in his chair, gesturing with his knife.

"I'm better than 'e is. And, ye've seen me in battle, I'm good with a musket."

"I've seen ye hidin' behind the main mast more often than not."

Walter wiped sweat off his brow as he tried to think of what would make him a good captain, a better captain than Roberts.

"Well, anything else, Commander?" Ethan asked long and drawn out.

"I can bring us more booty," he replied at last.

Ethan set his back against the chair and pointed the knife at Walter. "That's a tall order. How do ye think ye'll be able to fulfil it?" Walter didn't know how to respond, and Ethan didn't wait for him to think of something. "The only way for you ta become captain is to gain the support of tha crew. Right now, yer nothin' more than a whinin' babe. Ye talk big, but yer an earsore. Now why don'tcha piss off? I'm tired of listenin' to ye."

Walter gritted his teeth, but didn't say anything. He got up and left the group. *I'll show 'em. I'll find a way; I just need the right opportunity. I'll be captain one way or another.*

"Captain, the *Fortune* is signalling us," a crewmate yelled from the crow's nest. He was gazing through a spyglass into the wide open ocean. He moved the spyglass in another direction. "There is a ship North by Northwest."

"That must be the ship," Bartholomew said to no one in particular. "Helmsman, move us one point west."

"How can you be sure that's the ship we're after?" Hank asked.

Roberts smiled. "Just a feeling."

"Another one of your feelings. Of course."

"You don't doubt me?"

Hank shook his head. "Just as a cat never falls on its back, you almost possess a sense for which ship has the best haul. Six months and twenty ships later, your feeling has been there more often than not. I don't know where you get it, if it's luck or some gift from God, but you have it." He turned his attention to one of the sails. "Ugh, they got the jib rigging all mucked again. We're losing speed." He left to yell at the crewmates working the sails, leaving Roberts alone.

A gift from God? Not likely.

After the jib was freed, and the sails in a more optimal position, the *Royal Rover* started catching up to the *Fortune*. The *Fortune* was well ahead of them, however, and quickly caught up to the enemy ship.

Bartholomew Roberts' Justice

Roberts took out a spyglass to observe the *Fortune*. "What are they doing?"

"What's wrong?" Hank asked after coming back from the sails.

"*Fortune* isn't slowing down for us to catch up. I think they intend to attack."

"Surely you jest?" Roberts handed Hank his spyglass. He peered through the spyglass to the ships in the distance. "Damn," he cursed, then he gave the spyglass back. "Didn't you say you left Walter in charge of *Fortune*?" he asked.

"Yes, and I gave him explicit instructions not to attack until both ships were close. I was hoping to force them to surrender without loss of life."

"Not today, it seems."

"He must have lost control of the ship to the crew. His men are more bloodthirsty than they let on in front of me. I should have left you in charge of *Fortune*." Roberts clenched his fist.

"No use beating yourself up about it. If we can catch up the enemy may still surrender when they realise it's two against one."

Roberts nodded and commanded the men to work harder to improve the speed of the ship. When *Fortune* was close to the other ship—the *Decadence*, he hoped—*Fortune* released the black sail denoting it being a pirate vessel.

"Drop the black!" he yelled to the crewmate in the crow's nest.

The man climbed up a few feet of rigging rope to the very peak of the main mast and unravelled a rope holding in place a small black sail. When the crewmate finished untying the rope the sail revealed itself.

The black sail, newly chosen by Roberts since his taking command of the *Royal Rover*, pictured a crude representation of himself on the left, and the skeleton of death on the right. The two were holding onto an hourglass in the middle of the flag. The flag was mirrored on the main mast of *Fortune* as well.

Fortune was closing in on the firing range of the *Decadence*. Roberts peered through his spyglass at the two ships. He was able to see them clearly, and the *Royal Rover* would catch up within twenty minutes at their speed.

Perhaps Decadence will see our black flag as well and surrender without a fight.

The sound of cannons indicated the battle had begun. Roberts focussed his spyglass on the *Decadence* and he could see billowing smoke from its side.

So much for that.

Fortune and *Decadence* fired back and forth at each other. The larger *Decadence* was firing more cannons, but the *Fortune* was able to hold its own. *Decadence* stayed in one spot while firing, whereas *Fortune* moved away and towards the enemy ship in tune with the cannon fire. *Fortune* was able to hit *Decadence* more often than the opposite.

The sounds of the cannons thundered over the ocean and boomed in Roberts' ears. Because of the *Royal Rover*'s distance there was a slight delay between cannon fire and the sound reaching him.

As they advanced, the smell of smoke overtaking the sea air became ever more apparent. To Roberts that smell was all too familiar, and caused a stir in him he was loath to say he enjoyed. Battle came naturally to one of his size and stature, and as much as he wanted to avoid the activity, when he was in the thick of it he couldn't help but enjoy it on some level.

We're almost within firing range now, yet they haven't stopped. He turned to Hank. "Tell the men to fire a few warning shots at the enemy."

"We're too far away for it to be a credible threat, Captain."

"I understand, but *Decadence* has taken several hits and they know we're getting closer. Perhaps if we remind them of our presence they'll throw down their arms."

"Right," Hank replied.

Hank told the gunners above deck the plan, then went below deck to tell the rest not to open fire when the cannons fired from above. Once everything was ready, he gave the order to fire.

Three shots were fired in succession which landed in the water about a hundred feet from the starboard stern of *Decadence*. Plumes of water shot up from where the cannonballs fell.

Roberts watched the other ship through his spyglass. He could see the crew furiously running around the deck yelling orders, grabbing weapons and preparing for battle on the starboard side. He was able to find the captain, and recognized him as the man he'd met in the tavern. At the angle *Royal Rover* was he wasn't able to see the name of the ship, but now he knew it was the right one.

He noticed the captain and another older man in a heated argument. The captain pointed to the *Fortune* and the *Royal Rover* in between a flinch when a cannonball hit his ship. The other man seemed to be trying to reason with the captain. After a moment, the captain rubbed his face and turned around to his crew. They slowly stopped their frantic activity, and the cannon fire ceased. The man who was arguing with the captain handed him something Roberts couldn't see and then squeezed his shoulder. The captain nodded and then waved a white flag above his head towards the *Fortune* on the port side, and then did the same on the starboard side.

Yes. Now Fortune just needs to cease fire. Roberts turned his attention to the *Fortune*. He wasn't able to see the men aboard very well, but he could see the activity on deck easing, and the cannons eventually stopped firing at *Decadence*.

"Helmsman," Roberts called. "Bring us next to the enemy ship." The helmsman turned the wheel of the ship, pulling them in tighter to be in line with *Decadence*. "Men, prepare to board. Just because the enemy has surrendered doesn't mean we let our guard down."

Over a tense twenty or so minutes, the three ships furled sails and slowed down in tandem. Once their speed was sufficiently reduced, *Fortune* and the *Royal Rover* pulled up next to *Decadence*, tied the two ships together with grappling hooks, and then laid down gangplanks.

The crews of *Royal Rover* and *Fortune* boarded *Decadence* with weapons drawn. Roberts pulled out his sword and approached the gangplank.

"Hold for a moment, Captain," Hank said. Roberts turned and walked over to him. "What will we do about Walter?"

Roberts glanced over across the *Decadence* to the *Fortune*, and noticed Walter wringing his hands. "We can deal with him later. For now, we need to give the impression of unity and strength. Any weakness could be exploited."

Bartholomew Roberts' Justice

Hank nodded and pulled out his own sword. Together, he and Roberts crossed the gangplank to the *Decadence*. The crew was gathered in the centre of the ship and dozens of guns and swords were pointed at them to keep them stationary.

Roberts took a good look at the crew in front of him. The majority of the men were very young, and appeared to be inexperienced. Their hands were not yet calloused enough to be considered seaworthy. He approached one of the young men to examine his hand, and, sure enough, there were jagged, bloody cuts characteristic of rough rigging rope digging into the palm.

No wonder the battle was easy. Two-thirds of the crew are greenhorns. He eyed the gathered men and eventually found the captain. The man he had been having an argument with was sitting next to him, whispering in his ear. The captain was young as well, and the other man looked to be the oldest and most experienced of the bunch. *Perhaps the captain is also new to this.*

He rose to his feet and walked over to the captain. When he approached, the captain recognized him.

"You," the young man said, rapidly standing up.

Some of Roberts' crew stepped forward, weapons drawn. He held his hand up and they stepped back. "Yes, me."

"My father will hear of this when I return home, and you will hang for this."

Roberts chuckled. "Ah, so that's how it is. Your father's influence is what gained you this contract for goods, not any hard effort on your part. It explains the young men in your crew, and this old man being your mentor." He pointed to the man still sitting and the enemy crew around him. "You have to pay more for more experienced sailors, which would have meant less for you in the end." He raised his sword and place it under the chin of the young captain. The captain backed up a few short steps. "Or possibly more in this case," he chuckled. "Tell me, what makes you think you'll be returning to your father?" The captain visibly gulped as he stared at the blade on his chin. Roberts turned to his crew. "Search the ship and take everything of value you can find. This vessel's goods are now ours."

"Have fun while you can," the young captain said, his neck extended to avoid the point of the sword. "You'll be swinging from the gallows soon enough, pirate."

"So much the better," Roberts replied. "I used to be a sailor like the men in your employ, making low wages for hard labour while others gained the profit. Now, I have liberty and power, I take from people who have more than enough to spare, and spend it on the pleasures in life alongside my crew who do the same. If I die from this life, then so be it. My motto shall be to take as much as I can from people like you, and live a short and merry life."

3. EYE OF THE BEHOLDER

Roberts was on the deck of the *Fortune*, standing above two dead bodies amongst the wreckage from the previous fight. Though the inexperience of the *Decadence* crew helped, *Fortune* had not been able to escape unscathed.

He knelt down next to the bodies. "Do we know who brought them aboard?" he asked Hank, who was standing behind him.

"No, but I imagine we'll find out soon enough."

"Though these women had a less than desirable profession, they were still innocents. They shouldn't have been involved in this fight, nor paid this price. First young boys dying from powder accidents, and now this." Roberts shook his head. *I thought I was free of innocents dying under my care.*

The dead women were prostitutes by their dress and had been brought aboard before setting sail.

"Could you run by a vote with the commanders on punishing those who brought these women aboard?"

"What about Walter?"

"No vote is necessary, as, if I recall correctly, decisions relating strictly to battle fall under my jurisdiction as captain. It stands to reason that the punishment for not following orders in battle should be my job as well."

Hank nodded. "I'll run it by the other commanders just in case, but you have my support. We wouldn't have any casualties if Walter followed orders." Roberts smiled and nodded before Hank left to talk with the commanders.

"Oh, Hank, wait a moment," he yelled before Hank was halfway up the ladder. Hank turned around. "We should return to the island to sell our stock."

"Isn't that dangerous given that the *Decadence* is from there?"

"We cut their sails which should slow them enough. We'll have enough time to sell the goods, and if not we can leave on the morrow. Another reason I'd like to go back is so I can return these women to their families. They deserve that much, at least."

Hank wore a solemn smile before he nodded and returned to his task.

Roberts picked up one of the women in his arms and took her to the surgeon's room at the stern of the *Fortune*. After placing the first woman on a table, he brought the other woman in.

He took a wet cloth and cleaned their wounds as best he could. After the blood was clear he wrapped the wounds on their arms and legs, and stitched the clothes so the wounds weren't visible. After the women were as presentable as he could make them, he put a few drops of scented oil on them to stave off the smell of gunpowder and decay, then wrapped them in a loose cloth.

He left the surgeon's room and returned to the top deck of the *Fortune*. He glanced around at the crew busily taking stock and moving the sails around to give them more speed. His eyes eventually settled on the man he wanted to talk with—Walter Kennedy. He pointed at Walter and beckoned him over.

After a moment of hesitation Walter shuffled over to Roberts. "Yes, Captain?" he said meekly.

Bartholomew Roberts' Justice

"Come with me to the surgeon's room," Roberts commanded, trying to restrain his anger from bursting. "We need to discuss something in private."

He didn't wait for Walter to respond and went down the ladder to the lower deck, expecting him to follow. He entered the surgeon's room and when Walter joined him, he closed the door.

Walter went to the other side of the table. Roberts lifted the cloth off the women and gestured to them.

"What do you see?" he asked.

"Prostitutes," Walter replied.

"Innocents." He stared at Walter, who seemed to physically cower at his gaze.

"Well, whut do ye want me to do 'bout it? They're dead."

"It's not about what I want you to do. It's about what you should have done. They should not have been brought aboard, and if you followed orders and not attacked the ship before we were close this wouldn't have happened. Whoever brought these women aboard will be punished, but ultimately you are responsible."

Walter was silent for a moment before he objected. "Well, I cannot help it if tha men disobey me. If yer lookin' fer someone ta blame, Ethan was the one who brought them aboard and instigated the fight against that ship. He's the one ye ought to be yellin' at."

"I will investigate your claims, and if Ethan was the one who brought these women aboard, then he will be punished accordingly, but I say again you are still responsible for the men attacking *Decadence*. You say you want to be a captain, yet when given a chance to command you can't keep your men under control." He sighed. "You're only getting half shares of today's haul, and you'll no longer be in command of *Fortune*. You'll be back on *Royal Rover* until you're cleared for command again." Walter opened his mouth to object. "No," Roberts said, holding his hand up. "You had your chance. Now leave me."

Walter's mouth was a line, but his jaw clenched as he gritted his teeth in anger. He left the surgeon's room in a huff.

Later in the day, Hank finished his investigation and found several people who corroborated Walter's story involving the women who died. Ethan was the one who'd brought them aboard from a brothel on the island. The commanders also gave permission for Roberts to mete out punishment to him.

Roberts called him to the surgeon's room where the women still lay. When the two entered, he closed the door behind him. Ethan stood on one side of the table with his arms folded.

"Whut do ye want?"

Roberts pulled back the cloth covering the faces of the women. Ethan's face didn't change, but when he glanced at the women he visibly tensed.

"Do you have anything to say about these women?"

Ethan stopped glancing at the women's faces long enough to stare daggers at Roberts. "Nothin' in particular."

Roberts sighed and pinched the bridge of his nose. "Then you leave me no choice but to leave you at half shares for this haul."

"To hell with this."

"You'll return to full shares after our next raid."

Ethan gripped the table tightly while leaning forward. "Whut for? Some bitch whores died? Whut of it? No one cares if they died."

Bartholomew Roberts' Justice

Roberts' rage burned inside him. "God cares for all his children. These women died through no fault of their own. They have families just like us, and those women at the brothel will mourn for them. The fact you cannot see that explains exactly why you brought them aboard: You didn't care if they died. If this happens again, trust me when I say I will not care if you die."

"Is that a threat?"

"Take it however you want."

"Tch." Ethan let go of the table and stormed out of the room.

Roberts leaned on the table and stared at the faces of the dead women he didn't even know the names of. *Why did I bring up God now of all times?*

As Roberts and Hank strode down the street, passersby stared at them. It was midday and the streets were crowded, but the men and women parted for the pair. Confused whispers met his ears as he passed, but he paid them no heed.

The two each carried in their hands the body of a young woman wrapped in cloth—the two women who'd died aboard the *Fortune*. They were taking them back to the brothel they belonged to.

Upon arriving at the brothel and entering the establishment, they were greeted with even more confused looks. Roberts scanned the crowd of women and men in the run-down house. Men of all stations were patrons and women of all ages were catering to them in the lower floor which functioned as a tavern of sorts. Stairs led to an upper floor with rooms for privacy.

Jeremy McLean

"I need to speak with the madam," he said for all to hear.

An older woman strode down from the upper floor and over to them. Her brow was cocked slightly as she glanced at the bodies they were carrying. "Yes?"

"We need to speak in private, miss."

The madam gazed at the bodies once more. "Yes, of course. Follow me."

The madam turned around and went up the stairs. Roberts and Hank followed. She entered the first room at the top of the stairs and held open the door for the two men. After they were in the room, she closed the door.

"I can imagine what this is about. Show me their faces, please."

Roberts moved to a nearby bed and laid the woman on it. Hank did the same. They removed the cloth off the women's faces and stepped back to allow the madam some room.

She approached the bed with a pained expression on her face. She touched one woman's cheek and examined them.

"Stupid girls," she whispered. "How did they die?"

"They were smuggled aboard my ship. There was a battle and they died when they were hit by wood splinters."

"I told them never to set sail on a ship, but they never listen to me." The madam took a cloth out of her pocket and wiped the hair away from the women's faces.

"Do they have any family?" Hank asked.

"They're sisters, but their parents died long ago. We were their family."

Roberts glanced at Hank, then at the madam. "Then this rightly belongs to you and the other women." He reached into his pocket and pulled out some gold coins.

"What is this?" the madam asked.

"They shouldn't have been on our ship, and as captain I am to blame. This was for their families, and as you are their family you deserve this. I know this doesn't help with the loss, but I want you and your girls to have it."

The madam pocketed the gold. "Thank you, sir. I will make sure the rest of the girls see this." She opened the door for them to leave. As they left, the madam spoke with one of the girls outside the room. "Jean, fetch Pastor Sean and tell the girls not busy with clients to come up here."

Roberts stopped in his tracks. *A pastor?* "Excuse me? Why are you calling a pastor?"

"Women of our nature can still have faith. Luckily, there is one pastor in this city who practices what he preaches and prays for all sinners."

A pastor praying for harlots? I've never seen such a thing. Roberts turned to Hank. "You go on ahead, make sure the goods are sold and the ship prepped to leave." Hank nodded and exited the brothel. "Would it be alright if I stayed?" Roberts asked.

"Why? If you want some time with the girls you'll need to pay more."

"No, it's not that. I wish to speak with this pastor afterwards."

The madam nodded. Women from the brothel filtered into the room steadily. All were shocked when they saw the women who'd died, and before long many of them were shedding tears. After a time, the pastor entered and was greeted by the women.

"What are all the tears for, dearies? You missed me that much, have ye?" he asked with a smile. He was an older man with a Scottish accent which had softened from age. His frame was average, and his hair was beginning to grey. He had an air of fatherly authority, unlike the regal attitude Roberts was familiar with in other pastors.

"Father Sean," one of the women called through her tears.

The women parted to allow the pastor to see. Pastor Sean glanced at the bed, and then walked over to it. After a moment of silence, he turned around and smiled to the group.

"It appears the sisters are having a right old nap now, aren't they?"

One of the women gave him a confused look. "But, Father, they're dead."

"Not so, my child. They are merely sleeping, but not the same kind of sleep you or I have each night. Though, your sleep might also be a bit different than mine." The women laughed. "There, now that's better. You see, in this kind of sleep only the Lord can awaken them. Don't weep because your sisters are sleeping right now. Be happy that they will soon be with the Lord, at His table."

Roberts recalled a similar conversation he'd had with a man aboard *Royal Rover*. A crewmate had died shortly after he joined, and Roberts told a friend of the deceased the same thing Father Sean did.

"But what about their sins? They died before they could tell you."

Father Sean's smile turned into a frown, but not an angry one. "That is true. Well, what can we do about that?" The pastor smiled. "Can anyone tell me?"

"We can pray for them?"

"Correct, dearie. So let's all join hands and pray for Hannah and Suzan."

Bartholomew Roberts' Justice

Father Sean and the women of the brothel all joined hands and prayed for the women who died. Roberts didn't join in holding hands, but he couldn't help reciting the Lord's Prayer. After finishing the prayer, Father Sean had his own words specifically to ask forgiveness of Hannah's and Suzan's sins.

After the prayer was finished, the pastor continued to console the women and bless them. He was kind and compassionate, just like a fatherly figure.

After the pastor was finished talking with the women of the brothel, Roberts approached him. "Father, could I speak with you?"

The pastor took a step back as he looked him up and down. "Oh my, the Lord certainly blessed ye, son. You would be right at home in Scotland. Come, walk with me and we can talk."

He and the pastor left the brothel and walked in the street together. As they passed the citizens, many greeted the pastor with smiles and called his name. Father Sean returned their smiles and greetings in kind.

"So, what is it that troubles you?"

"Well, before that I wanted to say I've never seen a pastor praying for prostitutes before. Why do you preach to them?"

The pastor laughed. "Why would I preach to those without sin?" Roberts was taken aback by the implication. He never thought of it that way before.

"We are all with sin, and equal in the eyes of God. We all also have an equal chance for repentance and a change of lifestyle. Just as Jesus did, I preach in the hopes that sinners will change."

He and the pastor reached a small building with cross-shaped windows on the front. The building was simple and plain with no steeple as found on many other churches. The church had no door and was open for all to enter as they pleased.

"Come inside and we can talk in private."

He followed the pastor into the church. Inside there were rows of pews and at the front a stand for the pastor to preach from. On the wall at the back was a large window in the shape of a cross to allow light to enter.

The pastor went to the front and sat down in one of the pews. Roberts joined him. "So, what is troubling you, my son?"

He hesitated, trying to find the right words to explain what he wanted to say. "What does the Bible say about slavery?"

The pastor scratched his chin. "In the Old Testament it instructs on how slaves should obey their masters, and how they should be treated. In the New Testament, it reinforces slavery. In the book of Luke, Jesus made a parable out of a slave disobeying and being punished. Does this answer your question? I can't help but feel there is more to this than simple slavery."

Roberts glanced around. "What if a slave is mistreated? I previously worked on a slave ship, and many died because of neglect. And beyond that, men are profiting from these deaths."

The pastor nodded. "Ah, I see. You cared for the slaves, did you?" Roberts nodded. "Well, the Bible does say if a slave dies in the care of the slave owner then they are to be punished. I am loath to admit it, but I feel the way slaves are treated nowadays is far and away from how Moses or Jesus thought they should be treated." The pastor shook his head. "As for profiting from this business, the Bible clearly says the desire of money is the root of all evil. If these men are profiting by way of sin, then God does not approve. That you are not working on a slave ship now is commendable."

"But how can God allow these people to continue to profit? How can God allow evil to continue?"

The pastor laughed as if Roberts was a child. "God gave us life and free will to choose what we wish to do. God is allowing all of us the chance to find him naturally. Think of this Earth as His test. At the end of your life, you will be judged for your actions. It is certainly unfortunate that many suffer at the hands of evil men, but this is not God's doing. Only man is to blame."

Roberts balled his fist. "So what can we do when we see these evil men committing sin? Talking to them—preaching to them—does nothing. I cannot stand by while they kill the innocent. The women you prayed for today died at the hands of men like that."

"I can understand your frustration, my son, but the path of the righteous is one free from vengeance. Vengeance is for the Lord, not for man."

"What about when God sent the Israelites to war against the Midianites? They were sent by God to kill them because of the sins they committed."

The pastor hesitated. "Yes, that is true. God, through Moses, commanded the Midianites be put to death. That was a war, however, not a premeditated murder."

"So, if I am a soldier then killing is alright?"

The pastor raised his brow. "Are you a soldier now?"

Roberts scratched the back of his neck. "In a sense."

"No man is righteous as all men sin, and no war is good, but if war can prevent further evil then it is just to participate. That was why God commanded the Israelites to wage war against the Midianites. You must think deeply on your enemy and see if they truly are against God and his teachings. Only then will you know if your war is just."

Roberts folded his arms in thought. *As a pirate, do these rules still apply? If we free mistreated slaves and steal ill-gotten gains from the rich, is it actually acting out God's will?* Roberts thought of his departed friend from whom he'd borrowed his name. *Were you right all along, Bartholomew? Is being a pirate like Davis truly acting out justice?*

"Thank you, Father Sean, you've given me a lot to think about." Roberts rose to his feet and the pastor joined him. "I think now I need to buy another Bible."

He turned to leave, but the pastor stopped him. Father Sean reached into his robes and pulled out a small Bible. It was similar to the one he used to own: leather-bound, worn from use but well kept. Father Sean handed him the Bible.

"Take this one."

His mouth went agape. For a moment he couldn't think of the words to say. "I can't, this looks to be something precious to you."

Father Sean nodded. "It has served me well, but I feel you might need it more than I. There are always more Bibles I can use."

"Thank you, Father Sean. For everything."

"You are welcome, my son. I hope you find the answers you are seeking, and may God bless your endeavours."

Roberts smiled. "I hope he does as well."

He left the church and made his way back to the docks. As he walked, he leisurely thumbed through the new Bible in his hands. Its pages were worn, but it was clearly loved and cared for. None of the pages were ripped or torn despite the edges being curled and the ink slightly faded. It gave a faint smell of mint, and he found a mint leaf hidden on one of the pages, possibly functioning as a bookmark.

He stopped in his tracks to inspect the last pages Father Sean had been reading. He was trying to guess what the Father was reading when he found something which spoke to his current state of mind.

'The lions do lack and suffer hunger, but they which seek the Lord, shall want nothing that is good.' Roberts smiled. *Have you been providing for me this whole time?*

"Roberts, there you are."

He looked up to see Hank running over to him with a concerned look on his face. "What's wrong, Hank?"

"I went back to the brothel and you were gone, so I've been searching for you. I got wind you've been outed. We need to leave, now."

"Right." He took one last look at the Bible and put it in his back pocket. It felt snug, but comfortable, natural. "Let's move on to a new adventure," he said with a smile.

Hank smiled and the two ran through the streets back to their ships.

4. GOD PROVIDES

Walter followed Roberts and Hank as they carried the bodies of the dead prostitutes to the brothel. They were unconcerned with what was happening around them, so Walter didn't need to hide. The crowd parted for Roberts, as they often did. His large stature made it difficult for others to walk beside him, and he cast a large shadow.

Bastard thinks God's on his side. Soon he'll be out of the picture and I'll be captain. It won't be long now with Ethan on my side. A few more pushes ought to do, just have to find an opportunity…

When Roberts and Hank entered the brothel, Walter waited on the other side of the street. He watched the brothel entrance to see where they would go next. *They'll probably head to some tavern after this, and then I'll get them.*

After five minutes a prostitute left the brothel and headed further into town. Another five minutes passed and Hank exited the brothel alone and began walking towards the dock. Walter turned his face away in an attempt to avoid being seen.

"Walter," a voice called.

Walter turned and noticed Hank calling. *Damn.* "Hello, Mr. Abbot."

"What are you doing here?"

Walter's face felt hot. "Umm." He glanced at the brothel. "I thought I should pay my respects."

Hank nodded. "Good, good. The captain's in there

now. Make sure he's not too long, we don't know how long we have until we need to leave."

"Right, I'll keep that in mind."

Hank left Walter and went down the street back to the dock and the ships.

Now must be my chance. Roberts will probably be in there a while. I need to find an officer of the law.

Walter ran off to the centre of the town, rushing past the men and women in the streets and dodging the horses and merchants carts. He searched the signs on the buildings for the sheriff's office or a constable roaming the streets, something he'd never thought he would be doing.

After ten minutes of searching, he was sweating and breathing heavily. He reached a square and took a moment to stop running and search the crowd. The square was bustling with activity. People were talking and walking, several orators were littered about on small platforms speaking about news and politics, and children were running and playing around.

He eventually saw a man in a uniform walking around and being avoided by the citizens. He couldn't be sure, but he felt this was who he was looking for. He ran over and stopped short a few feet in front of the man.

"Sir, are you a constable? I know someone who needs to be arrested."

The man approached him, his eyes more alert than before. "What crime did you see committed, sir?"

He took a moment to catch his breath again. "There is a pirate, Bartholomew Roberts, at a brothel down the street. The brothel is called Stranger's Delight, I believe."

"I've never heard of this man, Bartholomew Roberts. How do you know him to be a pirate?"

Shit! What can I say that's believable? "I was uhh… on a

ship he attacked. He released us, but took all our goods."

The constable rested his hand on his chin. "Hmm." He scratched his chin for a moment as he stared at Walter, scepticism in his eyes.

Great, I get the one smart lawman.

"I'll question him about your claims. Show me the way to the brothel."

He let out the breath he was holding. "Follow me." He turned around and jogged back to the brothel with the constable following behind him.

At the brothel, he and the constable entered and scanned the room. He couldn't see Roberts anywhere. His gaze followed one of the women as they left a room upstairs with an open door. The woman had tears in her eyes as she left the brothel.

He must be up there with the dead whores.

He ran up the stairs and peered into the room. There were about ten women in the room crowded around a bed. They were talking amongst themselves and some were just staring at the bed. He couldn't see Roberts anywhere in the room.

"Oi, girl," Walter whispered to the closest woman. The woman turned around. "Where did that tall man go?"

The woman glanced around as she wiped tears from her eyes. The tears created streaks down her face through the dirt and grime. "I'm not sure. He was here a few moments ago."

"Does anyone know where the tall man who was here went?"

The women in the room turned around, then glanced about the room. After a moment they all shook their heads.

Damn! They must have been too preoccupied with those dead

bitches to notice him leaving. He left the room and the constable was waiting for him. "He's gone. No one seems ta know where he went."

The constable's mouth was a line. "Alright, you're coming with me so I can get more information on this Bartholomew Roberts. Something doesn't feel right about your story."

The constable reached out to grab Walter by the arm. He jumped back. The constable's eyes widened, then narrowed as he glanced from his hand to him.

The constable lunged at Walter. He hopped over a railing and down to the first floor. The constable peered over the edge of the railing. Walter fell on the wooden floor of the brothel and was scrambling to his feet.

"Stop! Stop, I say!" the constable yelled as he turned around and rushed to the stairs.

Walter was already on his feet when the constable reached the stairs, and ran towards the exit. The constable was halfway down the stairs. Walter rushed into the streets of the city, glancing this way and that, trying to determine the best way to run.

"Get back here!"

He ran to his right, towards the harbour. The constable was hot on his heels. The Irishman weaved through the crowds of people in his way. He glanced over his shoulder. Luckily, the constable was having as much difficulty getting past the crowd as he was.

He sprinted down side streets, behind buildings, and turned at every corner. He could hear the constable yelling behind him in pursuit.

Sweat poured down his face and he felt winded, but he kept running. His legs burned and his arms were getting tired, but he kept running.

Eventually, the sound of the constable faded until he couldn't hear him any longer. He was a few blocks from the dock when he stopped running.

Walter fell to the ground in a side street and caught his breath. He took out a kerchief and wiped his damp brow and forehead. After a few moments of rest, he approached the edge of the side street and glanced up and down the main street. He couldn't see the constable, nor any others he might have recruited, in the street. He let out a large sigh and headed back to the docks.

When he reached the *Fortune*, Ethan and his friends rose to their feet and met with him. They crowded around him, looks of anticipation in their eyes.

Ethan glanced this way and that. His eye next to the tattoo twitched, and he couldn't keep still. "So, did ye do it?"

Walter looked around and noticed several crewmen talking and doing busywork. "We should talk below deck."

Ethan nodded, and the group went down to the crew cabin. When they were in their usual spot, after removing some other crewmates, Walter explained in a hushed tone what had happened on his mission.

Ethan slammed his fist against the starboard planks. "Bollocks, Walter. Ye screwed us over."

Walter raised his hands. "We can still salvage this. We just need ta go ahead with the other plan."

"It's gonna be hard to convince everyone you deserve ta be captain when ye can't even get a simple job done."

"I can navigate, and unlike Roberts I won't take away yer shares when ye want ta have a little fun onboard the ship. Drinking, prostitutes, tell them they can have it all and more when I'm captain."

Bartholomew Roberts' Justice

Ethan stared at Walter as he bobbed his foot up and down. He had a scowl on his face, which simply wouldn't change. Eventually he let out a "Tch," before looking off to the side. "I suppose that'll do. We just need ta make sure our men are on the *Royal Rover* before this all goes down." He stared at the other men in the group. "You can handle that, right?" The other men nodded. "Alright, let's make you captain then, Walter." He stood up and put out his hand. Walter rose to his feet and shook his hand. Ethan pulled Walter in close and whispered to him, "Don't screw this up, or ye'll be swimming with Davey Jones. Ye hear?"

Walter nodded, but when Ethan and the others weren't looking he let out a large sigh. *What am I getting myself into?*

Roberts, Hank, Walter, and the other commanders sat in the mess hall at a large table discussing recent and future events. The *Royal Rover* and *Fortune* had both escaped before the authorities could find them, and luckily managed to sell some of the cargo in the short time they were docked.

"Alright, we're all in agreement about the division of shares?" Hank asked. The commanders nodded. "On to other business then. Roberts?"

Roberts nodded. "There's been a lot of shuffling around of the crew recently from the *Fortune* to *Royal Rover*. Normally this wouldn't be an issue, as we're all the same crew and it doesn't matter who works on what ship, but it's more than usual. Anyone have any idea what it might be about?" He looked at the commanders, but they all shook their heads. "No one mentioning grievances with crewmates aboard the *Fortune*? No?" He eyed Hank, but his number two shrugged his shoulders. "Walter, I know it's a sore spot, but do you think it could have anything to do with your move back to *Royal Rover*?"

Walter's face was spotted with sweat. "Possibly. Uhh… Ethan also moved over to *Royal Rover* again, and his troupe could have been a part of that move. From there it could trickle down to other crewmates who're friends with Ethan's friends."

Roberts nodded. "Understandable. Unfortunately, this has left *Fortune* understaffed. When we next reach dock we need to send some crewmates over to *Fortune*." He turned to Hank. "Hank, would you be willing to handle that?" Hank nodded. "Alright, let's put it to a vote."

"Ah!" Walter exclaimed. All eyes turned to him. "I can do that if you want."

Roberts raised his brow. "Why take on extra work? We've been on a ship together for a long time now, and let's face it: you'd rather be in your hammock than not." He smiled, and the other commanders chuckled.

Walter smiled slightly. "Yes, well, I feel the need to prove myself after my mistake on the *Fortune*. If you'll allow me, I'd like to have the opportunity."

Roberts was impressed. "Alright, all those in favour." The commanders replied with "Aye." "Then it's settled. You'll handle dividing the crew at the next harbour." Walter smiled. "Now, speaking of the next harbour, where should we head to next?"

The Commanders discussed options for travel, but none had any solid ideas on where to acquire their next haul.

"Well, there is one option," Hank offered after a bit of

deliberation. "We could head West, across the Atlantic."

"To what end?" Roberts asked.

"I've heard the Caribbean is mostly lawless and has many pirate havens. We could head there and see where it takes us."

Roberts rubbed his chin. "Having some stomping grounds would help against situations such as the one we were just in, but how is our food supply? Will we be able to make it?"

"I believe we have enough to travel to Brazil. We can make a stop there, stock up, travel the coast to see if we can find any ships to raid, then head on to greener pastures."

Roberts nodded. "Anyone else have other ideas?"

The other commanders didn't suggest anything, save Walter. "I think we should head north," he offered. "The Irish coast is teeming with small trading villages. We could make one of 'em a base and attack tha merchant ships which arrive. Once we're finished, England and Wales are a hop and a skip away."

"Sounds promising, but dangerous. The British Navy would always be hot on our heels if we stay there. Let's put it to a vote. All those in favour of Walter's plan?" Four commanders and Walter raised their hands. "All those in favour of Hank's plan?" Hank, Roberts, and five other Commanders raised their hands. "Alright, Hank wins the majority vote. We'll be heading to Brazil then."

With the course set, the *Royal Rover* and *Fortune* headed to Brazil. Along the way, when the wind was not in their favour and there was a lull of activity, Walter divided the crew and put men from the *Fortune* over to the *Royal Rover* or vice versa. He seemed overly enthusiastic about the activity, which Roberts found an improvement, given his recent poor attitude.

A week out from landing in Brazil the *Royal Rover* and *Fortune* were hit by a storm and blown off course. Luckily no one was injured through the ordeal, but they landed further south of Brazil than they'd anticipated.

The ships ended up near Ilhéus, so they decided to head there first to repair and sell cargo, and seek out prospects. What they found, however, was disappointing.

The harbour and land of Ilhéus was a venerable paradise. Covered in palms, greenery, and sandy beaches, pristine water and open skies, it was quite different from the eastern shores the crew was used to.

The disappointment was the size and state of the harbour. It was a small harbour with barely any room for large merchant ships. The harbour was littered with small sloops and smaller fishing boats, but nothing worth their time as far as Roberts was concerned.

After docking, Roberts left the *Royal Rover* to talk with the local harbourmaster and see if he could glean any information. He could see a bounty of people staring and pointing at the large ship in port.

Hank joined him and the two walked up the dock to land. They were met by a tanned man who waved to them. Roberts approached and put his hand out to shake. The man took his hand and shook it.

"Do you speak English?"

"Yessir, I am slow, but I speak for you."

Roberts nodded and set his hands on his hips, glancing around at the locals still enamoured by the *Royal Rover*. The smell of fragrant meats and coconut met his nose on the back of a wave of sea air.

"The locals seem surprised to see us."

The harbourmaster chuckled. "Yessir, big ships not

come here much."

Roberts glanced at the harbour's bevy of fishing ships. "I can see that." He shielded himself from the hot sun. "We were hit by a storm and had no choice but to land here. Our ship was damaged slightly and we have cargo to sell. We were hoping you would be able to accommodate us."

The local ran his fingers through his hair. "We can fix ship, but cargo…" The man gave a so-so gesture, rocking his palm side to side. "Better to sail north to Baía de Todos os Santos. Big port, many ships."

Roberts nodded with a smile. "Is there any anchorage?" The man seemed confused. "Charge for docking?"

The man nodded. "Ah, five real."

"Do you have any reals, Hank?" he asked.

"I believe so." Hank pulled out a coin purse and rummaged through it, eventually finding five reals he could give to the man.

"Thank you," Roberts said to the local, and then he turned around and returned to the ship.

"You seem to be a in a good mood despite not having any ships to raid."

Roberts laughed and stopped walking. "Well, let's just say I'm confident we'll find something."

"Another one of your hunches?"

"Before we decided where to sail next, I prayed to God for an answer to a question I had recently."

Hank raised his brow. "I haven't heard you talk about God in some time, and from what I recall when you first joined us you used to carry a Bible around with you. You haven't had that since… then."

Roberts nodded. "Yes, we lost too many that night."

"Aye, too many, too much, and some more than others." Hank gripped Roberts' shoulder with a knowing look in his eyes. "I never asked because it seemed like a private matter, but I'm curious: what's changed? Something that pastor said?"

Roberts scratched his chin. "You know, I lost my way because of all the horrible acts I saw committed by so-called men of faith. I thought that if God was with them then I didn't want to be with God." Hank nodded. "The pastor made me see that all men are sinners, but those who profit from evil will never win. I prayed for Him to show me whether what we are doing is just, or if we too are doing evil. I believe if God considers our cause to be just, then He will provide for us."

Hank smiled. "Well, it is certainly odd a pirate can say he is doing God's work, but I hope you find your answer soon." The two walked back to the ship, and when they approached, Hank let out a "Hmm."

Roberts smirked. "What?"

"I was thinking maybe instead of Bartholomew the Bear you should be called the Pirate Priest." He chuckled.

Robert laughed with his friend. "It does kind of roll off the tongue. I like it."

They boarded the ship and told the crew about where they were. It was decided they would repair the ships, perform a boot-topping to clean the barnacles off the ship above the water line, replenish supplies, and then head north to Baía de Todos os Santos.

Roberts ordered the whole crew to work so they could leave as quickly as possible, and in a few days they were ready to leave Ilhéus. They travelled along the coast of Brazil, soaking in the sun and gazing at the tropical locales. The relaxing time after the storm helped improve morale.

When the crew reached Baía de Todos os Santos, Roberts' first thought harkened back to the passage he saw in the Bible he received from Father Sean. *They which seek the Lord, shall want nothing that is good.*

In the harbour of Baía de Todos os Santos were at least a hundred ships of all types and sizes. Large merchant vessels were entering and exiting the claw-shaped bay, but the sight that caught Roberts' and the crew's attention the most were forty-two ships flying the flag or coat of arms of Portugal. The ships ranged from sloops-of-war to small frigates like *Royal Rover*. Most carried cannons, and all of them spread out in the harbour either docked or anchored in the water.

Hank glanced at Roberts. "God provides," he commented.

Roberts chuckled. *God provides.*

5. THE PIRATE PRIEST

Roberts entered the third tavern in his search for someone associated with the Portuguese ships in the harbour. The first two times he had no luck, and he was beginning to run out of steam. Asking everyone who seemed receptive the same questions over and over, and burning through money to purchase drinks for said people, was wearing on his mind and coin purse.

He approached the tavern bar and sat down on a stool. "Ale, please. Dark."

The woman working the bar nodded, and then filled a mug with dark ale from a cask behind her. She handed the mug to him and took his payment. He took the ale and turned around in his seat while he took a swig. After a foamy head, the dark ale went down smooth. It tasted of roasted nuts, a hint of coffee, and dark chocolate like what he ate in Príncipe. It reminded him of his departed friend Bartholomew, and of when they'd tried the roasted cocoa in Príncipe. Roberts would never forget that fond memory for as long as his mind allowed him to.

The tavern he found himself in this time was very open with a second-floor indoor balcony and many tables. In the corner of the room, away from the balcony, was an open space for dancing and a fiddler playing a

Bartholomew Roberts' Justice

merry tune for all to hear. It was certainly more upbeat than the other taverns he'd visited, and his mood quickly shifted as he tapped his foot to the rhythm of the fiddle.

"Pretty good, ain't he?" someone asked next to Roberts.

Roberts examined the man who talked to him. He was an older gentleman with dark complexion and a short salt-and-pepper beard. He appeared to be a regular at the tavern by his look. "Yes, quite lively indeed."

"When did you arrive in the bay?"

"Just today. I'm a merchant by the name of Bartholomew Roberts."

"Gabriel." The man moved his ale into his off hand and went to shake Roberts'.

Roberts returned the handshake. He scanned the room, and could see a few men in what he thought could be dressed-down formal attire, but he couldn't be sure.

"Tell me, Gabriel, those men there, do they hail from the fleet of Portuguese ships in the harbour?"

"Yea, they are. The one on the left is a captain of some sort. If he can call himself a captain."

Roberts chuckled. "You seem to not like him."

Gabriel laughed. "Arrogant sod keeps mentioning the ships in their army and how they're transporting supplies."

"Hmm," Roberts replied. He leaned over and nodded his chin at Gabriel. "How would you like to help me and stick it to him?" He gestured to the captain with his ale.

Gabriel leaned in. "I'm listening."

"I have half a tonne of gunpowder I need to sell. The only problem is my supplier gave me shite for powder. Works maybe half the time because the mixture was shoddily done. Too much saltpetre. If you and I can make friends with this captain, get him tanked, and get him to buy my powder, I'll be ahead, and when his crew tries to use it they'll be in for a surprise. What do you say?"

"You want to know how to bring people with money to you?" Gabriel asked.

"What?"

Gabriel produced a pack of playing cards from his pocket. "The prospect of winning more money, and arrogance. When you start to lose, lose loudly," he said with a sly smile.

Roberts couldn't help but smile as well, and the two sat at a table adjacent to the Portuguese men. Not being familiar with card games, especially those played for the purpose of gambling, Roberts didn't need to feign losing. The further into the game they got, the more boisterous the two became, and other people crowded around the table to join the game.

"And I win again, gentlemen!" Gabriel shouted over the other patrons.

"Ugh!" Roberts yelled, throwing down his cards. "I swear you're unbeatable, old man."

"So you don't want to play again?" Gabriel winked at Roberts.

Roberts noticed the wink. "I tell you, I cannot. My pockets have run dry. The Lord is my witness, my wife

Bartholomew Roberts' Justice

will have my head."

"Oh come now, I'm sure she'll be happy when you return with double the winnings. Double or nothing."

Roberts shook his head vigorously. "You are too good, and I'm on to your tricks. I'm simply not adept enough at this game to stand a chance." Roberts rose from his chair.

Gabriel held out his hand. "Hold, hold now. How about I let someone substitute for you, to win you back your money? Would that make it fair?"

Roberts smiled, understanding the old man's plan. "Well, I suppose that would be fine, but who will spot for me?" He and Gabriel eyed the other people who were playing with them, but they declined, having seen Gabriel's skills.

Roberts turned around to the Portuguese table. "Oi, you there," He called, pointing to the captain. "I'll split my winnings with you if you can beat this old man at a game of cards."

The captain waved his hand and shook his head. "Find someone else."

He leaned forward. "Come now, I need some help here," he pleaded.

The captain looked annoyed. "I said find someone else, vagrant."

Roberts turned around, defeated. When Gabriel looked at him he shrugged his shoulders. He was out of ideas.

"You heard the man, he's too afraid he'll lose too, so you must find someone else," Gabriel said loudly.

The crowd laughed at his comment.

"What did you say?" Roberts heard the captain say angrily behind him. He smiled at Gabriel, and Gabriel smiled back.

"Oh, that was nothing need concern you, sir."

The captain rose from his chair and approached Roberts' table, with his crew joining him soon after. "It does concern me. You said I was too afraid to lose."

"Well, that isn't something to be ashamed of, sir. Not everyone can be good at these games, it takes a certain skill…"

"I assure you, I have the skills, and I could beat you any day."

The crowd was getting into the argument, and sought to rile the two parties up even further. They were doing most of the work for Roberts and Gabriel. The alcohol might have contributed as well.

"Well, prove it then, young man," Gabriel chided.

Roberts rose and motioned for the captain to sit in his seat. The captain took the offer while staring down Gabriel. "Deal, old man."

Gabriel nodded, and the game began. He lost the first game, but with a few words from him and Roberts, they kept playing. Roberts was behind the captain the whole time, cheering him on and getting him progressively stronger drinks. From his new vantage point he was able to see Gabriel was manipulating the cards somehow. He made sure if the captain won it was by a small margin, which gave him the pleasure of reward but still retained his competitive spirit. Over time Gabriel lost more frequently until he called a stop to the game.

Bartholomew Roberts' Justice

"Well, you seem to have bested me, sir. I had you pegged wrong. I'm all out of money now."

The Portuguese captain, now fully drunk, with his subordinates sleeping on the floor or at their tables, laughed heartily. "Thas right, I win."

Roberts slipped some money from the table into his pocket and then shook Gabriel's hand with the money hidden in his palm. "It was a good game, and I thank you for allowing me the help."

Gabriel shook his hand and took the offered money. "The pleasure was all mine," Gabriel said with a smile before he left.

"Where ya goin'? We're no done yet."

Roberts took some more money off the table and pocketed it, then shoved some in the captain's pocket. He then picked up the captain and put his arm over his shoulder. "Come now, sir. Let's get you a drink on my ship."

The captain looked around. "Ah, what 'bout my men?"

"Don't worry about them, they're taking a nap. They'll join us later."

Roberts carried the Portuguese captain from the tavern all the way to the *Royal Rover*. Several times the captain burst out into song, or tried to brawl with him, but he was able to coax the man back into following him. Eventually he made it back to the ship before midnight.

Roberts, with the help of Hank and a few others, took the captain to the crew's quarters and tied him up. "Thanks, men. I'll take it from here." He knelt down to get almost eye level with the captain. "Captain, you're with those forty-some Portuguese ships, aren't you?"

The captain nodded with far too much movement. "Yea, we're waiting fer two big men-o-war to get us to Lisbon."

Roberts cocked his brow and glanced at Hank. Hank wore the same confused expression on his face. He turned back to the captain. "Why do you need a warship escort?"

"Cause we got the goods. Can't be losin' the king's jewels." The captain instantly sobered up, and his eyes widened. "Oh, I shouldn'ta said that."

Roberts smiled at Hank. "Now, Captain, we're friends, right?"

The captain smiled. "Yea, good old friends now."

"Good, good. As a friend why don't you tell me the name of the ship carrying those jewels?"

The captain's mouth made a line and he shook his head. "I shouldn't."

"What's the harm in telling little old me? I'm a simple merchant," Roberts coaxed. "I want to know so I can know who to trade with." He pulled the money from the bar game. "Tell you what, I'll give you this for helping me find these people to trade with. You help me, I help you, and you help your superiors. We all win."

The captain gazed at the money with lust in his eyes. "I'm helping you?" Roberts nodded. "Ship's named Providence."

Roberts smiled and patted the captain on the shoulder. "Thank you, friend." He rose to his feet. "Hank, gather our twenty best fighters. We're about to go for a swim."

Bartholomew Roberts' Justice

"It's now or never, Walter," Ethan said in a hushed tone. "Hank was left in charge and there are maybe twenty men not with us on the *Rover*. We can take 'em."

Walter was sweating. The thought of what Ethan wanted to do was wracking on him. *This is what I wanted, wasn't it?*

"Boys, leave us and get the men armed." The other men left the corner of the crew cabin. Ethan stood up and stared down at Walter. "I told ye before if ye want ta be captain ye need the support of the crew. The men aren't gonna follow some pussyfooted landlubber jus' because he knows how ta navigate and lets em do what they want. Ye want ta be a leader, ye need ta lead. Show the men yer worth a damn, or else they won't follow you."

Walter looked up at Ethan. *Ethan's right. He has respect from the men because he takes it, not because they give it to him.* He stood up and grabbed a cutlass in his hands. "Let's go," he said confidently.

Ethan and Walter left their usual spot, and Walter could see men lined up in the crew cabin. Each man held weapons in hand and watched him as he walked past them. Some of the men nodded to him and others hooted or slammed their fist on their chest. There was a nervous energy in the crew cabin, and despite all the people and the hooting it was quiet. The pressure he could feel kept his feet moving. He kept thinking on Ethan's words and saying to himself *I must do this*, and *I will be captain*, over and over.

He reached the ladder. He could see the moon's light coming in through the opening to the main deck. He took a deep breath and went up. The men followed behind him and before long over a hundred men were on the main deck of the *Royal Rover*.

Hank was on the main deck with about twenty other crewmates waiting for Roberts to return. When men emerged from the crew cabin with weapons in hand he approached Walter.

"What is the meaning of this?" Hank asked while gingerly placing a hand on a cutlass at his belt.

"I am taking over this ship. Roberts is captain no longer."

Hank raised his brow. "There was no vote on this. You have no authority to take these actions." The twenty men on Hank's side gathered around him.

"The only vote which matters is the vote of the crew, and Walter has ours," Ethan stated. The crew hollered in agreement.

"Tell me this then: Who was the one who gave you revenge for Captain Davis while this coward ran?" Hank seethed, pointing at Walter. "Who was the one who's found us more booty in the past six months than we've gotten in the past three years combined? Do you think Walter would break into a prison to save you from the noose? Perhaps you should ask your new captain what he plans on doing when he is captain before you continue with this folly."

The crowd of mutineers whispered amongst themselves and Walter could feel the hot breath of doubt on his back.

"I'll tell you one thing I will do," Walter said, stepping from the crowd and turning around to face them. "I won't attack a fleet of forty-two Portuguese ships, putting ye all in danger in the process. Ya think the King of Portugal'll let us alone after we steal his jewels?" The men nodded and the whispers seemed to be more in his favour. "I'll tell ye something else I'll do: I'll let ye drink and bring as many whores aboard as ye wish. Life on a ship as a pirate is hard enough as it is. Ye already put yer life on the line, not bein able to wet yer stick is too much to ask of ye." The crowd was becoming more vocal and turning back to his side. "I want what all of ye want: a nice, easy life where all pleasures are laid out before us. Roberts wants ye ta be good Christian pirates who abstain from the comforts life provides. I'll tell you now, and again if ye stand by me as captain, that will not be how things are run from now on. Who's with me?"

The crowd unanimously cheered for Walter.

"Enough of this," Hank said.

The sound of a cutlass being unsheathed rang out in the midst of the cheers, and all other sounds died out for a fraction of a second. Walter's eyes widened and he turned around to see Hank rushing towards him with his cutlass out.

The sound of steel rang out. Hank's blade was deflected. Walter spun around and saw Ethan beside him. Ethan had protected Walter from Hank.

Hank backed up a few paces, and the twenty men with him drew weapons. The crowd behind Walter and

Ethan stepped forward, but Ethan called out for them to stop.

"Hank," Ethan said. "Ye fought next to us over the years, just as all of ye did. We don't want ta fight. Leave the ship and we'll let ye go. We owe ye at least that much."

Hank scanned the eyes of the hundred plus men in front of him ready to fight, then at the men next to him. Walter could tell that the twenty men at Hank's side were scared, but still ready to fight if he chose to.

Hank lowered his weapon. Soon after, all the men on the *Royal Rover* lowered their weapons. "You win."

Hank and the other crewmates on Roberts' side entered a dinghy on the starboard side of the *Royal Rover*. Ethan and a few others lowered the dinghy into the water.

"Roberts will never forgive you for this," Hank yelled when the dinghy was halfway down.

Walter stared into Hank's eyes. "I know," he replied.

Roberts and the twenty men he took with him to raid the Providence were in two longboats paddling back to the *Fortune*. He could see the crew on the deck, waving and calling their attention. There was more activity than he expected in the middle of the night, but he was glad for it, as they needed to leave immediately.

The crew manoeuvred the longboats to the side of the *Fortune* as rope ladders and rigging for the dinghies were thrown down.

Bartholomew Roberts' Justice

Roberts climbed a rope ladder and jumped over the side. "Gentlemen! God has seen our cause as just, and we shall not be wanting for some time." He wore a great smile on his face, and his hands were at his sides. As he looked at the crew he noticed Hank there. "Hank, what are you doing on the *Fortune*? Were you not on the *Royal Rover*?" He scanned the harbour, but could not see the *Royal Rover* anywhere. "Where is our sister ship?" He noticed the dejected demeanour of his crew.

"The *Royal Rover* was taken," Hank stated.

"By whom?" Roberts asked quickly.

Hank looked at Roberts with fury in his eyes. "Walter Kennedy."

Roberts was taken aback. "Why would he do such a thing? Tell me we were found out and he had to escape," he pleaded.

"I cannot, as the truth is far worse. I reckon it was because of his desire to be captain not moving forward. He rallied crewmates to his side with promises of doing away with your commands. Letting them drink while on duty and having their precious whores onboard. They let the crew and me go, and then took the ship north."

Roberts ran his fingers through his hair and turned away from Hank. He ambled to the port railing and leaned against it. He gazed at the water lapping against the side of the *Fortune*.

"Captain, will you be alright?"

After another moment, Roberts turned around with a smile on his face. "I am perfect, Hank. With this I finally have my answer."

Hank looked confused. "I understand what you

mean, Captain, but our ship was just stolen from us. We're pirates, yet we were stolen from? Is that not as absurd and aggravating as it sounds?"

Roberts laughed, causing the crew to give him strange looks. "God has provided for us in more ways than one."

He went over to one of the newly raised longboats, pulled a heavy chest out, and brought it over to the crew of the *Fortune*. He lifted the opening of the chest, and in the pale moonlight over them the contents of the chest shone bright gold like nothing they had seen before.

Inside the chest was filled to the brim with gold coins. The crew of the *Fortune*, having not seen the contents until just then, began laughing hysterically and cheering. The twenty men who joined him were smiling as they brought the other chests on board. They opened them one by one until twenty-four chests of gold coins and various jewels glittered on the deck of the *Fortune*.

When the hysterics seemed to die down, Roberts explained himself. "Not only has God seen fit to give us this bounty, but with the crewmates who saw fit to betray us gone we have all these riches to ourselves." He raised his hands up to his sides. "We are God's chosen!"

Roberts sat in a comfy chair in the captain's cabin. He was reading from his Bible, the well-worn but cared-for Bible he'd received from Father Sean. The ink was slightly faded in spots, the pages curled, but there was life in that book. He could tell so much about the Father from where the book was worn the most, almost as if the Father was right at his side.

A rap at the door grabbed his attention. "Come in," he said.

Hank entered the captain's cabin. "Howdy, Captain. They're ready for you out here."

"Thank you, Hank," he said, standing up.

Hank nodded, and it seemed like he was about to leave, but closed the cabin door instead. He stared at the deck. "Captain, I don't believe I had a chance to say it before…" He paused, and then looked Roberts straight in the eye. "I'm sorry about what happened with Walter. I should have fought him, I should have chased after the ship with *Fortune*. I should have…"

"Hank, stop," Roberts commanded. He walked over to Hank, his friend, his first mate, and placed his hands on Hank's shoulders. "You prioritized the lives of the crew, which was the right thing to do. Davis would have done the same."

Hank smiled, thinking back to his former captain. "'Worry about you and your comrades first' he always used to say." Hank chuckled. "I miss him."

"I do as well." Roberts paused a moment to think of those who had passed on, the lives that had influenced him so much and brought him to where he was today. Davis, Delliger, Bartholomew. "God's judgement will be brought upon Walter, just as Judas in the past and just as we did the Governor of Príncipe. He will not escape justice." He let Hank go. "Now come, the crew is waiting." Hank nodded.

Roberts and Hank exited the crew cabin, and went to the main deck of the *Fortune*. The whole crew was gathered, waiting for the captain to begin. He stood on the quarterdeck, and the crew sat down on barrels or on the deck.

"Welcome to the first of many Bible studies to come. Let's begin, shall we?" Bartholomew Roberts cleared his throat and opened the Bible he held in his hands. "God created the heaven and the earth. The light and the darkness…"

THE END

OTHER BOOKS BY THE AUTHOR

The Pirate Priest Series:

BARTHOLOMEW ROBERTS' FAITH

BARTHOLOMEW ROBERTS' JUSTICE

BARTHOLOMEW ROBERTS' MERCY

BARTHOLOMEW ROBERTS' SPIRIT

The Voyages of Queen Anne's Revenge Series:

BLACKBEARD'S FREEDOM

BLACKBEARD'S REVENGE

BLACKBEARD'S JUSTICE

BLACKBEARD'S FAMILY

The Collection Series:

BLACKBEARD'S SHIP (Includes Books 1&2 of The Voyages of Queen Anne's Revenge & The Pirate Priest)

BLACKBEARD'S BLOOD (Includes Books 3&4 of The Voyages of Queen Anne's Revenge & The Pirate Priest)

ABOUT THE AUTHOR

JEREMY IS CURRENTLY LIVING IN NEW BRUNSWICK, CANADA WITH HIS WIFE HEATHER, AND THEIR TWO CATS, NAVI AND THOR.

Jeremy's first foray into the writing world was during a writing competition called NaNoWriMo, where the goal is to write a certain number of words in the month of November.

After completing the novel he started, and some extensive rewrites, he felt it was worthy of publishing and self-published his first novel, Blackbeard's Freedom in September, 2012.

After writing over ten books under two names, his passion for writing hasn't wavered over the years, and hopes to one day make it his primary career.

Let everyone know what you thought of his novels by leaving a review. He loves getting feedback on his books, and loves to hear from fans of his work.

Want to pirate one of Jeremy's audiobooks? Visit www.mcleansnovels.com/faith-audiobook-offer for a free copy of one of his audiobooks.

www.ingramcontent.com/pod-product-compliance
Lightning Source LLC
Chambersburg PA
CBHW070758050426
42452CB00012B/2395